In memory of my dad who introduced me to frogs and toads,
my Uncle Tony who sang to me about them, and
my Aunt Helen who loaned me her bucket to catch them

—J. R.

For John

—M. K.

Henry Holt and Company, LLC
Publishers since 1866
175 Fifth Avenue
New York, New York 10010
www.henryholtchildrensbooks.com

Henry Holt® is a registered trademark of Henry Holt and Company, LLC.
Text copyright © 2007 by Joanne Ryder
Illustrations copyright © 2007 by Maggie Kneen
All rights reserved.
Distributed in Canada by H. B. Fenn and Company Ltd.

Library of Congress Cataloging-in-Publication Data
Ryder, Joanne.
Toad by the road : a year in the life of these amazing amphibians /
by Joanne Ryder; illustrated by Maggie Kneen.—1st ed.
p.   cm.
ISBN-13: 978-0-8050-7354-6
ISBN-10: 0-8050-7354-X
1. Toads—Life cycles—Poetry. I. Kneen, Maggie, ill. II. Title.
PS3568.Y399T63 2007   [E]—dc22   2006015361

First Edition—2007 / Designed by Laurent Linn
The artist used watercolor on hot-pressed watercolor paper
to create the illustrations for this book.
Printed in the United States of America on acid-free paper. ∞

10 9 8 7 6 5 4 3 2 1

TOAD
by the ROAD

A Year in the Life of These Amazing Amphibians

by Joanne Ryder
illustrations by Maggie Kneen

HENRY HOLT AND COMPANY • NEW YORK

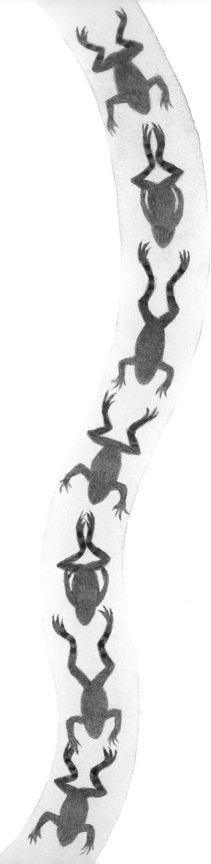

Spring–Summer

Summer

Late Summer–Fall

Winter–Spring

SPRING–SUMMER

The Pond's Chorus

One toad,
One song.
Two toads
Sing along.
Three toads,
Better yet.
Four toads,
A quartet.
Five toads
Catch five flies.
Six toads
Harmonize.
Seven toads
Hum higher.
Eight toads,
Quite a choir.
Nine toads
Pause . . .
And then . . .
Ten toads
Start again.

Springtime Singers

Sitting knee-deep
In the cool water,
We toads hum along
High and clear,
Puffing like balloons,
Blowing out our tunes.
Other toads can hear
And hop near.

Everyone who listens
At sunset
Grins a little
When old toads sing—
Filling up the night,
Trilling soft and light,
Our cheery voices
Welcoming spring.

In the spring, male toads wake up from their winter's sleep and head to ponds and puddles. First a few sing, then other males join in. Female toads listen and meet them to breed.

Escape

Toad eyes,
Tower high,
Blink and stare,
Spot and spy.
Sly snake
Sliding low,
Gliding closer . . .

Off I go.

Toads have large eyes near the top of their heads and good vision. Many animals won't eat toads because they protect themselves with a poison that tastes bad, but snakes can eat them without harm.

Tadpole's Surprises

I *splish* and *splash!*
I dive and swim.
My tail flicks like
A fish's fin.
I'm sleek and shiny,
Smooth and black.
Hey, *legs* are popping
Out in back.
These legs are fun.
I'd like some more.
Hey, look at me.
Now I've got *four*.
My tail! It's *shrinking*.
Hey there, *stop!*
It's *gone*. . . .
   I'm leaving.
    I can HOP.

 Toads may lay thousands of eggs in long strings. The eggs hatch into fishlike tadpoles. Tadpoles gradually change into tiny smooth-skinned toadlets and hop to shore to live on land.

Old Toad's Warning

Toadlets,
Beware!
Please cross
The road
With wide-eyed care.
Be sure to look
This way
       and that.
Then hop,
Don't stop . . .
Or—
Splat!
    You're flat.

Toads often migrate in large numbers to their breeding ponds and have to cross roads as they come and go. Many toads get run over by cars and trucks. But caring groups of people help save toads by putting signs at toad crossings to warn drivers, and even by building fences to direct toads into tunnels made under the roads so they can cross safely.

Raining Toads?

Raindrops
Plopping
On the ground.
Toadlets
Hopping
All around!
Is it raining
Teeny toads?
   No . . .
We're just
Skipping down
The roads.
Today is
Toadlet Moving Day!
Farewell, pond.
We're on our way!

Toads sometimes take advantage of a rainy day to move from pond to land. Great numbers may hop across the ground as the rain falls. It looks to some like it's raining toads!

An Ever-So-Silly Song

We toads are wild and wacky.
We are a silly bunch.
We never brush our teeth
Before or after lunch.
We haven't any teeth,
And we haven't any hair.
So if you need a comb,
We won't have one to share.

Both frogs and toads are amphibians—cold-blooded animals many of whom live part of their lives in water and part on land. Generally, frogs have smooth skin; toads have dry, bumpy skin. Most frogs have teeth, and most toads do not. But, like all amphibians, frogs and toads have no hair, scales, or feathers.

SUMMER

Summer Days

A game with sun
I play all day.
Sun sneaks up close,
I dance away.
Sun's breath flares hot.
Sun's touch can scorch.
But I am safe
Beneath the porch.

Zap, Zap

My tongue is a tool—
Far better than most—
For catching my breakfast,
Though I shouldn't boast.
It's long and it's swift
And it's covered with goo.
I flick it at cricket
And stick him with glue.

A toad waits and watches an insect or worm creep near. Then it flicks out its sticky tongue to catch its prey. The toad swallows its meal whole and then wipes its mouth clean.

Yummy Bugs

One bug . . . Two bugs . . .
Three bugs . . . Four . . .
Fill up my tummy, please.
I'd like a little more.
Five bugs . . . Six bugs . . .
Seven bugs . . . Eight . . .
Whoa!
I can't believe
How many
Bugs I ate!

Toads are helpful animals in a garden. They eat plant-eating insects, caterpillars, and slugs. One toad can eat thousands of insects each year.

Toad's Summer To-Do List

Sleeping . . .

Sleeping . . .

Sleeping . . .

Now it's time to hop.

Skipping . . .

Skipping . . .

Skipping . . .

Now it's time to stop.

Eating . . .

Eating . . .

Eating . . .

Now my work is done.

Singing . . .

Singing . . .

Singing . . .

Morning, neighbor sun!

  Frogs have long legs and can leap far. Toads have shorter legs; they walk or hop.

Toad in the Garden

Roof and floor.
Roof and floor.
What could I ask for?
Not much more.
Just . . . one fat fly
Buzzing by.
Not too fast.
Not too high.

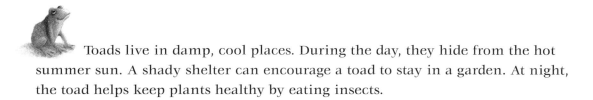

Toads live in damp, cool places. During the day, they hide from the hot summer sun. A shady shelter can encourage a toad to stay in a garden. At night, the toad helps keep plants healthy by eating insects.

The Thunder Toad

Bounding
From cloud
To cloud.
Thunder Toad
Grumbles,
Rumbling loud.
Small toads hear
His rainy song,
And in the mud
We sing along.
We rumble low.
He grumbles high.
Toad in the garden.
Toad in the sky.

Frogs and toads are most often heard giving their advertisement call at breeding time. But some also give distress calls, alarm calls, and rain calls.

Toad's Drinking Game

In the rain
Others hide,
But I'm
Quite pleased
To sit outside
In a little
Mossy rut—
Eyes open,
Mouth shut.
Here I drink
The rain within,
Clear drops
Trickling
Through my skin.

 Toads can absorb moisture through their skin. So they "drink" by sitting in the rain, a puddle, or a damp spot—with mouths closed!

LATE SUMMER–FALL

Chilly Chums

We share
The cool morning,
Bee and I.
I nap and rest.
He waits to fly.
He's grounded
For now,
Just warming
And sunning,
Until he can get
His motor running.

Marvelous Molting

Some folks fill up
On fancy food
And then go on a diet.
That doesn't sound
Quite right for me,
So I don't think I'll try it.
When my dry skin
Starts feeling snug,
I shed it
Like a sweater.
I yank it off
Over my head.
Ahhh . . .
My new skin
Fits much better.

 As toads get bigger or grow older, they shed their skins. This is called molting. Underneath, toads have new, soft skin to grow into. Toads don't waste their castoff skin—they eat it!

Rah, Rah, Toadlets!

We're short.
  We're brown.
    We're bumpy.
We're young.
  We're strong.
   We're lumpy.
We're proud to be
Toads, wild and free.
  We're short.
   We're brown.
    We're bumpy.

By fall, the tiny spring toadlets have grown. Their skin is no longer smooth. Like older toads, they have bumpy or warty skin. If you touch a toad, you should always be very gentle, then wash your hands. Don't worry, you can't catch their warts! 27

Hide-and-Seek Days

The sky above is falling—
Floating scraps of red and brown.
It's hard to find a bit of earth
Where sky has not come down.
My roof is now a crazy quilt
I snuggle underneath
And dream of happy days gone by
Beneath a curling leaf.

A toad's color and bumpy skin provide camouflage—they help the toad blend
into shady hiding places so it can avoid predators.

Just Fooling

When you wiggle near,
Creeping close to attack,
I just tumble over,
Lie flat on my back.
Oh, no . . .
I've stopped breathing.
I'm silent. I'm dead.
Or am I just waiting
Till you turn your head?
Now up pops a leg . . .
Then another—
Flip, flop!
Can you see my wide grin
As I *hop* . . .

hop . . .

hop?

A toad will play dead to defend itself. Some predators won't eat prey that appears dead. As soon as the toad feels safe, it will turn over, hop off, and escape.   *29*

Anticipation

Caterpillars
Are spinning.
Birds are
Soaring south.
Chipmunk races
Down a log,
Beechnuts in her mouth.
Everyone
Seems busy
Going his own way.
But winter lasts
A long, long time.
So I'll enjoy today.

Some animals leave as winter draws near or prepare for it by storing food.
Toads do not. They will sleep all through winter—burrowed underground.

Fall Toad

Fall blows
Up the pumpkins
Into bright balls.
Toad
Sits hushed
Among them,
Hearing no calls.
Grass is dry.
Weeds are high.
Fall chills
One and all.
Toad is feeling sleepy.
Toad is feeling
Fall.

 By fall, most frogs and toads have stopped singing. They won't call again
until spring.

WINTER–SPRING

Good-bye Song

Good-bye, grass! Good-bye, tree!
Good-bye, pumpkins, house, and bee.
Good-bye, mud. Good-bye, sky.
Sun and moon and stars,
Good-bye.
I am moving underground,
Kicking, flicking, digging down.
I am leaving. Watch me go.
Sheltered safe from ice and snow.
Hello, darkness. Good-bye, day.
May all stay well while I'm away.

Intermission

Winter glides quietly.
Thunder toad
Sleeps in his cloud.
Snowflakes
Dance silently.
No bird is singing out loud.
Rain *pitter-patters*
Yet no toad is trilling along.
Only wind whistles,
Piping a shivery song.

Toads have strong hind legs and dig their own burrows to hide from danger,
extreme heat, and cold. Their hearts beat slowly, as they rest below the frost line,
safe from snow and icy winds.

Toad's Winter To-Do List

Sleeping . . .
Sleeping . . .
Sleeping . . .
Is what I like best.
Dozing . . .
Dozing . . .
Dozing . . .
So much time to rest.
Dreaming . . .
Dreaming . . .
Dreaming . . .
Nothing else to do.
Yawning . . .
Yawning . . .
Yawning . . .
I'm awake.
Are you?

Toads awaken and leave their burrows as the weather warms. Young toads will stay nearby on land. When toads are several years old, they return to ponds to sing and breed.

Spring Again

I stretch my legs
And try to leap,
A little stiff
From months of sleep.
I hop and hop
Through leafy doors.
In spring,
            I spring
On mossy floors.

Toads generally live alone. But at breeding ponds, many toads, and later toadlets, may be seen together. A group of toads is called *a knot of toads*. A group of frogs is *an army of frogs*.